POETRY now

IMAGES IN WORDS

Edited by

Andrew Head

For Stella,

With Friendship + Love,
from
Josie Brew! x
(Jo. Mc. Pherson)

First published in Great Britain in 1999 by
POETRY NOW
1-2 Wainman Road, Woodston,
Peterborough, PE2 7BU
Telephone (01733) 230746
Fax (01733) 230751

Copyright Contributors 1999

HB ISBN 0 75430 582 1
SB ISBN 0 75430 583 X

FOREWORD

Although we are a nation of poetry writers we are accused of not reading poetry and not buying poetry books: after many years of listening to the incessant gripes of poetry publishers, I can only assume that the books they publish, in general, are books that most people do not want to read.

Poetry should not be obscure, introverted, and as cryptic as a crossword puzzle: it is the poet's duty to reach out and embrace the world.

The world owes the poet nothing and we should not be expected to dig and delve into a rambling discourse searching for some inner meaning.

The reason we write poetry (and almost all of us do) is because we want to communicate: an ideal; an idea; or a specific feeling. Poetry is as essential in communication, as a letter; a radio; a telephone, and the main criteria for selecting the poems in this anthology is very simple: they communicate.

CONTENTS

THE VISITATION

Satan came to visit me
He sat upon my shoulder
And the more I looked at him
The more I grew colder

I said in nervous voice to him
Why do you visit me
He said to take your soul away
It is your destiny.

L Chandler

CHRISTMAS

A warm feeling of love as we sit by the fire, surrounded with
chestnuts and warmth from the fire.
Snow beating on the windows, children playing games,
everyone excited as we wait for Christmas day.
As Christmas day draws near everyone is filled with joy,
everyone laughing with fulfilment of their joy.
Sandwiches and carrots lying side by side
along with the sherry and lager nearby.
Santa will be here soon, and all the children in their beds,
trying desperately to see, the man that's dressed in red.
Christmas day arrives children everywhere
waking up early and running down the stairs.
Opening their presents is the best of all, watching their faces glow
with presents that are small.
Opening the biggest present brings tears to their eyes
as they see the gift before them and wonder how and why!
Christmas dinner is in the houses moving from room to room,
then Christmas puddings' aromas like a fragrance of perfume.
A warmth in the air, a glow in the dark,
children outside singing carols in the park.
Throwing snowballs, scrubbing faces making people laugh,
today's the day that hate and jealousy are pushed right back.
Snow crunching as we walk, leaving footprints to and fro,
giving like a different meaning as we see it white with snow.
Christmas day is nearly over but still hopes are high,
as everyone is happy with the stars in their eyes.
When children go to bed Mam and Dad relax,
knowing that their children are happy in their sacks.
Little children are happy, but that's still not enough
they still haven't seen the man they love so much.
Christmas day is full of love, giving and receiving
everybody's happy and everyone is pleasing.

Donna Hamm

THE SEA SNAIL

I wish I had a sea snail that could sing sweet songs,
About shells that could sing shalom for so many hours.
It would be called: Singer, Sweety Pie, Silent or Sparkle,
But the most thing I care about is I want a winkle!

Morgan McHale-Dill (6)

THE DAY THE WORLD CRIED

I was in Canada the day the world cried
when we heard the sad news that Diana had died.
Within a matter of hours, there were carpets of flowers
wherever Diana had been,
where she had not Canadians never forgot,
in their hearts she was a queen.
She was queen of their hearts who had found love at last,
and for her flags were lowered half mast.
The ships in the harbour from whichever country they came
flew their ensigns half mast just the same.
Union Jacks were spread over the ground and masses of
flowers laid upon them, pictures of Diana wearing her crown
were tenderly placed among them.
Books of condolence were opened all over,
people queued for hours to sign,
The pages were filled from cover to cover
with messages of love on each line.
Some had met the lady who cared,
and spoke of the pain and suffering she shared,
The touch of her hand, the encouraging smile,
when her own heart was breaking some of the while.
She was loving and giving and made life worth living
for those who needed her love,
she will reign in the hearts of Canadian people
as she smiles upon them from above.

There was anger, frustration, despair and distress,
as we all mourned the death of a beloved princess.
Who was at fault, who was to blame?
Who should be bearing the guilt and the shame?
Who did permit this relentless stalking,
which in Canada is a criminal offence,
stalking in packs a defenceless lady,
for that there can be no defence.
What kind of law allows this destruction,
and *why* didn't someone take previous action?

Had it not been for stalking, selfishness and greed,
a change of chauffeur there would not have been need.
On the day of the funeral at four in the morning
Canadians were watching TV,
they were shedding tears and expressing fears
for Diana's sons and her family.
Everything stopped in the stores in the malls,
for two minutes' silence for the Princess of Wales.
When her life was portrayed
the National Anthem was played,
she was held in the highest esteem,
as long as she lives in the hearts of the people
she will always be a queen.
Such honour and respect I did not expect
from a country so far from my own,
Whilst the British were grieving
the whole world was seething
and the UK did not grieve alone.

Sheila Hansford

TEMPUS FUGIT

If our time on earth is the mere blink of an eye
on the timescale from the planet's birth
and we let so many chances slip by
whilst the soothsayer proclaims the end is nigh!
All in their own time!
A drop of rain is all it takes
to send a million spores way up high
and one seed in ten thousand
to make a flower grow.
But all in their own time.
Like a tree to reach maturity
some like the life of a human.
Sixty years may pass whilst another a mere ten
and the fly that from birth to death
forty eight hours and nothing left!
All in their own time
like the gears in a clock all at different speeds
but every one determining one final outcome
even people like everything in the universe entire
there is a time relative to infinity and all contained within.
Of course infinity has no sides, no walls, no end
and did not begin and to waste it is apparently as sin!
At least we're told again and again.
So if you really want to waste some time
it's OK it's relative you see
daydreaming is constructive, necessary even
if it highlights the warning sights
and if you stop and stare awhile you can see them . . .
But all in *your* own time.

R James

KAIJA

I love you more and more each day,
I hope our love will never fade away.
Being so far apart,
It really breaks my heart.

Till August we must wait,
Then we open love's gate.
Till then my dear,
Stay calm and never fear.
Love will always come through,
My darling, I do so love you.

Peter E Jones

UNDER BRACKEN THATCH

To lie down and sleep
Under bracken thatch,
And slumber deep,
With mental balm, on nature's soft down patch.

A million beads of glistening dew
Fall upon forehead and cheek,
Exquisite colours of a crimson hue,
From the falling sun, grow weak.

A hint of frost within the air
Clear distant sounds of night
Breaths freshness to the nostrils' hair,
Shimmering stars in heaven's roof burn bright.

Emerald carpet by my side
Rustling blades that ripple and sway
Stretching down to the woodland far and wide
Wave to the passing day.

The hoot of the owl after twilight
Distant forest begins her whispering song
Croaking ponds and crickets' tunes delight,
All enter the terrestrial harmonic throng.

Down time's dark paths to shadows deep
Through the melting hours my mind alights
With memories, dreams, God's gifts I keep
As I slumber tranquil through the night.

I slowly ascend to a conscious state
Grey, phantom light upon the hill
Fluorescent shafts through cumulus gates
Disturb the gloom that once was still.

Dawn's scarlet cloak in the eastern sky
Gilt, blazing trumpets, herald the morn,
As ten thousand red roses burst on high
Lend a wash of gold to the waving corn.

The valleys, the fields, the hills, forests too
Erupt with music that fills the ear,
The singing lark climbs to the blue
Nature's chorus begins the melody clear.

I stir and rub my heavy eyes
And lift my head to greet the day,
Pick up my rucksack and arise,
With a strolling step I walk away.

Away from the spot that once was my bed
Down to the river a fish breakfast to catch,
Then on to the hills that lie far ahead
Come nightfall, I'll sleep, under bracken thatch.

Alan Brydon

BSE

Birth was not the start of life
It shattered a warm and cosy world.
The chill was cutting as a knife,
Into the hands of humans hurled.

Supposed to have no thoughts, no soul,
Yet with hazy mind I dream.
What of my mother's milk so pure
Now I'm fed by machine!

Day in, day out behind these bars,
I feel there must be more than this.
Just once I tasted fresh green grass
Yet even that's not what I miss.

Forced apart from one another
Hemmed in by concrete walls
No comfort found in friendly herds
Our grief is in our calls.

But worse than this, our nourishment
Comes from a hostile source,
Cannibals these men have made us
Nature banned from taking course.

One day I see a fellow prisoner
Dragged by human past my stall
Slipping, tripping on the concrete
Nothing done to break his fall.

A crack like thunder through the barn
Exceeded only by the shriek
The carcass slowly dragged away
The stench of blood begins to reek.

Still we eat this noxious stuff
Or starve, our main decision.
In this hell our terror grows
With death our only vision.

Head feels light, my brain a sponge
I fall onto my knees.
Mind is crazy as I lunge,
It's called Mad Cow Disease!

Surely this cannot go on
Without horrific penalty.
The final price will not be paid
By us, as they shall see!

Sarah Case

SEPULCHRE

I breathe a little deeper,
The air, it smells much sweeter,
The pain's becoming greater,
The light is getting brighter.
My heart beats slightly slower,
The breathing's getting deeper,
The pulse is growing heavy,
My mind begins the cleaving,
Of contact with my being,
My soul feels like it's leaving.
All is black, I cannot see,
All is silent, I cannot hear,
No arms, no legs can I move,
And the only smell is fear.
Oh, such bright, eternal light,
My eyes might burn with thee,
I can still not move a limb,
But now at least can see.
My family are dressed in black,
Appearing one by one,
Now sound has returned at last,
I hear sobs of 'Now he's gone.'
Is it me of whom they talk?
And if so why do they cry?
Proclaiming that I have gone,
Gone where - my God, where am I?
The darkness has returned,
I feel life draw to a close,
And suddenly know the truth,
Now, the battle I must lose.
Senses that I used to have,
Return to me I beg,
Or I shall be forever interred,
As my kin believe me dead.

Oh, voice so loud reiterate,
My cries of life aloud,
And fists of power once immense,
Pound hard to make a sound,
No avail, my cries of woe,
For life to return once more,
My coffin's being carried now,
By six good friends I'm bore.
I feel the drop as I descend,
And hear the first soft thud,
Of earth thrown on my early grave,
And now the shovelled mud.
Is covering the wooden tomb,
So, I can not escape,
And even though I'm still alive,
Death has become my fate.

Ashleigh Jane Fletcher

SPRINGTIME AT VOUNI

How still the sea,
How blue, how deep,
Seen from these ancient stones,
Two thousand years ago a house of kings
Set high above the ocean.
Graceful ruins now, they still retain
The aura of their former glory.

Cradled by mountains, kissed by flowers,
A tranquil carpet of anemones,
Deep violets and celandine
Lies at their feet.
A wide-eyed lizard
Darts from rock to rock,
Intoxicated by the noonday sun.
The air is humming with the sound of bees.

A lone bird calls to the wind,
The cool and gentle wind that bends the pines.
A wind that softens sadness,
Calms emotion, sharpens
Memories of things past,
Caresses the restless spirit.
We know what royal ghosts walk here,
When afternoon's pale moon
Hangs stark and cold in the clear night sky.

There is a peace about this place.
I came with troubled soul.
I will return again,
For I have felt its healing touch,
Glowed in its warm embrace.
I will return.
This place will make me whole.

Norma Fraser Reid

BO-PEEP

Coming home
in reverse?

Perhaps a
Bo-Peep thought
watching her sheep
wagging their tails
behind them!

Where else?

Unless,
suddenly,
everyone
began going
backward
yet still
going forward
having developed
eyes in their elbows -

now there's a thought!

Godfrey Dodds

PROMISE

Summer winked her eye today
As frosty trees stood still
Her faint warm grin touched winter buds
And promised soon comes spring.
Summer fluttered deep blue eyes
To warm the coldest heart,
She touched with just the softest touch
A sparrow and a lark.

Summer played a merry dance
On bushes white and cold,
She sent a burst of joy around,
As winter now grows old.
Summer left and winter stayed
But for a while did play
Our memories carry on the warmth
As summer tempts each day.

April Cook

THE MATHS LESSON

I was in my maths lesson today
My mind was far away
As the teacher was chalking
I was talking
And I didn't hear what she had to say

When she asked me a question
A simple one at that
The reason I couldn't answer
Is because I'm always having a chat

The class started laughing
Which made me feel thick
This is why I always get a cross instead of a tick.

Joanna Lock (12)

WHO CARES?

Nursing Huntington's a time of despair
few want to know, fewer even care.
Thirty five years of living in hell,
who can you turn to, who can you tell.
The whispers, remarks, and public sneers,
destruction of your family, in heartbreak and tears.
My body is broken, my legs are now wheels,
my brain is still active, and my soul still feels.
Once in a lifetime, that's all you can hope,
that someone still listens, understands,
and helps you cope.
Five years ago, this I must say
a knock on the door, a woman called Kay.
No sign of a halo, or hint of her wings
it is rather less than desirable, when she sings.
I should have noted, the presence of calm
as she lowered gently to take Andrea's arm.
In the knowledge of living with Huntington's,
your short life is an unseen hell.
Andrea, Nick and Justin in death's shadow cast its spell.
I have never before seen angel tears, descend as the glittering dew,
this is true understanding at long last, through and through and through.
No chore too small, no task too great, a woman to rely on.
A carer has rare reward, but her skirt hem is worth an eye on.
When Huntington's finally takes my wife,
an everlasting hole, will be left in my life
having to tell my kids the same,
our angel Kay will keep me sane.
The test of time will surely be,
tending my family, in the cemetery.
Man's pure greed, and self interest, a gross lack of care
through all our pain and anguish, our angel Kay is there.

No honour, no money, no words can I ever repay,
how Kay Gorden gets me through each and every day
I wish for all my Huntington's families they too
Can have their angel true.
My heart is with all the people, who lose their family to
Huntington's too.

Robin S Raines

MI GRANDAD'S FERM

Mi grandad were a fermer
when I were five thanooas,
but I were nobbut a learner
dressed I' swanky sormon clooaths

Mi grandad thewt ee wer' t' gaffer
o'er t' beaass an' pigs an' t' bern
till mi granny skriked wi' lafther
an' said oo wer' t' brain ont' ferm.

Place were wick wi dugs an' moggies,
they ed um to keeap daewn t' rats
an' it were one at ferm 'ands' 'obbies
to shaewt on um when e seen one in' t' lats.

Id were one o' my jobs to wesh shandry
used te tek aewt milk I steyl kits,
but ars-end were heigher than were 'andy
an' did newt but mucky mi mits.

I were freight tut deeath it t 'hen coite
wit thens o flappin thur wings,
I were fain to be tewd not to go theer
as I'd stop 'em fro laying an' things.

We ed te get beass it shippon
'cos they ed to be milked afore neet,
an they knew their own shop tween t' boskins
an t' way they cum in were a treet.

They o ed a name and responded
te names like Millie an' Meg,
when tha gave um thur provin an' fodder
they exchanged it fer milk fro' a bag.

Best job of o were Sat'dy kittin
when granny collected o' t' brass,
oo treighted mi te black puddins
an mi grandad some ale in a glass.

We left mi grandad still suppin,
'e were towd te find 'is way oam,
when 'is pals wuld put 'im it shandry
and tell t' thoss to tek 'im streight oam.

There warned much traffic I' them days,
an' Dolly new 'er way oam,
oo pulled t' shandry wi eighat any bother,
but then oo ed plenty o rooam.

Rex Cook

Bright Light

There's an empty space in my heart;
It hurts so much I want to cry,
I think of you day and night,
I hope to see you in the light.

S Laurie

DRUGS

Standing on a street corner,
Sniffing up the dirt,
Losing my life,
To the troubles of my world.

Down a dark alley,
Losing my livelihood,
To the others of this game,
Stealing my relief.

Dossing in the streets,
Wasting my life,
To the human killer,
Which is taking me out.

I've pushed my family away,
And I've lost my friends,
Except one,
The drugs.

Ashley Sheppard (14)

LIFE

In this world of war and crime
Work all day to earn a dime
Life through saddened eyes I see
World of no hope no destiny
No hope for this world
No hope in your life
Work all day for your kids and wife.

The people's war the Irish fight,
No one roams the streets at night
British soldiers rule by day
Is there no other way?

Streets of violence and of crime
The government has had its time.
Prisons filled with death and hate
Something must be done, before
It is too late.

War and crime must end right now
Nobody knows, quite how.
This world of ours must turn around
Or no happiness will be found.

Christopher Reek

MINERS

Across the hills - across the miles

The pits stand still, no miners around
The noise has gone, and that familiar sound,
The pit wheel that turned and is now gone,
The coal fields bare, where did we go wrong.
We, the miners, just stand and stare
Hands in pockets, in despair
The pride is gone, what do we do,
Lord please tell us what to do.

Jo

HERETIC

These clever clever poets
Make me sick
I write in real language
I want you to understand
I'm not saying you're thick,
But as my speech is plain
I am branded heretic.

This is world music
Painful to the ears
Hell's decibels.
But they don't like it
Those pretentious fools
They try and drown me
On their ducking-stool.

But I can walk on water,
See?
Those clever clever gits
Won't silence me.

Ros McCullain

My Mam

The world has many mothers
But none like mine.

The world has many mothers
But to mine, I could build a shrine.

She's looked after me and cared for me
For oh so many years

She's laughed with me and cried with me
And helped me through my fears.

Yes the world has many mothers
We all know this is true

The world has many mothers, Mam,
But God blessed me with you.

Linda Jones

BOOKS

Books are alive
they are in my room
they are destroying the earth
we're at our doom.

Coming through the ceiling
coming through the door
coming through the window
coming through the floor.

They are taking over my room
they're like giant flies
but what are they doing
they're taking over my eyes.

Jordan Honzik

POLL TAX FREE

Whether it's warm and dry or cold and wet
Rarely do I have anything to eat
To life I feel such a cheat
Everything to me becomes a threat
I live with rats, and clothes barely a thread
You and others snub me in the street
Is it just the fact I've got bare feet
Or that unlike you, I sleep not in a bed?
I don't have the faculty to live,
But the gift of being free.
If only one of you would care about me.
All I possess in life is the little you give,
All I want to be
Is accepted in society.

Karen Smith

UNTITLED

Oh pretty rose upon the wall
How you grow to be so tall
Stems outstretched climb to the sky
Your buds not yet open to the naked eye

Green leaves sway in the evening breeze
You're fourteen now and have grown with ease
You will go on forever I know
Throughout the seasons and the snow.

Dennis Russell

ANOTHER CHANCE

I was in an empty place
which filled with light and souls
that did not show, for in this space
was not nor could be substance;
and pain was taken from me.

Of the place there came a voice
that called, but not my name.
Far from me a quiet reply;
'Lord, I confessed all my sins.
Received mine absolution.'

Again the voice, 'But not of Me.
Who can save his brother?'
The silence pulsed, the far one asked,
'Lord, how can this be? What may
be done that I would be saved?'

Once more the voice, in sombre tones,
and this place flinched and feared.
'Too late. You are of the damned.'
The far voice wept, then faded
and deep sadness filled the space.

Then came my name! and the voice
within filled all my soul.
'And thou?' and I awoke, in
my own room. Another day
more time, another chance.

Alastair Gilmour

Upon The . . .

Upon the grains of sand,
On the ocean floor,
Once lived a turtle,
That now is no more.

Upon the tree tops,
High in the sky,
Once lived a sparrow,
Who always loved to fly.

Upon the soil of earth,
Lives a person called me,
Who always loved to write,
And now is 103!

Erin Gavagan (12)

SADNESS

As the sea of sadness surrounds,
The tunnels and passages of my heart,
Drowning all emotions,
In the great depths of sadness.

As the air tight cell of sadness comes down on,
The freeness of my happy soul,
All self esteem suffocating,
Away from all eyes under lock and key of sadness.

As the overwhelming power of sadness looms over,
The darkness of my creativeness,
Stamping upon all thoughts within my brain,
Crushed under the mighty foot of *sadness.*

Joe Yates (12)

ISLWYN PROSSER - MY MOTHER'S BROTHER

I remember him now, not as in the picture
on Mam's dressing table.
But then I didn't know him when he was young
I remember him when he was old.
When his hair was grey and growing wild
like the couch grass by the bog
And when his massive chest was bare
and he smelled of sweat, of coal dust and of beer.
I was a young man when he died
who saw through the smiles in his twinkling
blue eyes, to the pain.
Who saw how his teeth bit into his lips
behind his constant, crooked smile.
And I can't forget how his bristled chin
stung when I kissed him.
Oh, how I longed to fall on that cancered wreck
God knows I longed to cry dry tears for him
That I knew he could never cry even in pain
He had taken me, two running steps to one
up into the mountains.
Had taught me to swim and dip and dive
in the tingling pools of the distant rivers.
I can see his spirit now
whistling between the Bruce and the Prime Llewelyn Inn
flirting with the young wives on the benches in the park
haunting the 'shilling each way' shops he loved so well
and whistling home to a bungalow tomb
on a hill in Pant.

David Rees

FICKLE FIRE

The pain my pain
Let me tell you about my heart
About the flames that burnt it out
The naked heat
From head to feet
Flames liking at, but I couldn't see
The blackness that gets left by fire
Just my passions
That kept getting higher
But even the toughest get burnt to ashes
With every fickle flame that passes.

Cathryn Tideswell

THE MATCHMAKER

We talked about someone's desperation.
I couldn't think of anybody else who could help.
Being a gentleman, I thought you might obliged.
Will it work?
I believe so.

In midsummer day, we arranged our meeting.
Under a parasol, we had ice cold drinks.
Pleasant conversation went on.
My eyes sifted between you.
I saw you; you felt uneasy.

Before parting, you both kissed with half lips.
My feet went cold on the hot pavement.
A streak of jealousy crept in.
My God!
This is not good.

Talked about of having another meeting.
You wanted me to be there.
How could I?
It was bad enough to offer you.
I could not do the rest.

Actually I am frightened.
I am just putting it on a brave face.
The pain is within.

Our love is my consolation.
Not only comforting but also a solid one.
Hug me that I must not worry.

Pink Magnolia

LET VIOLINS PLAY . . .

Let violins play and guitars strum,
bees will buzz and
humming birds hum,
let hearts and minds alike entwine
with flowers perfum'd and sweet, sweet wine

and love gently whispering down
in floating coloured clouds
it's settled now, it's silken gown
around my world; and heavenly harps
begin to play
the conjured magic brings love this way.

No more! I cry, a bleated yelp
as heart strings flutter nonchalant;
succumbed by passion, stifled are my calls of help
blanketed by birth, the lumbering entity arrives
and Cupid's arrow bursts my heart and leads my
soul into eternity . . .

Ron Matthews Jr

DUNBLANE

The tears, they rolled and rolled
That fateful day a nation wept
Seventeen souls departed from
This life, they, call sublime
How can our minds
Be at rest
The day a nation wept?
We know there is earth
Is there a heaven?
Have the little angels
Of Dunblane
Forgiven that sickly man?
I do not know
I would like to think so
I could not.

C Vickerage

PEACE

Speak with earth upon your feet -
Silent path, between the sea and shore;
No footprints kindling pride,
Unwritten by the living song.

Give with empty hands
To those whose needs are full;
To the winds turn, and scatter
Your promise with the valley dew.

Gaze toward the moonless night
Blinded, by each starry light;
In darkness, your sleeping heart's dreams
Sail the beauty of the mind.

D Merrick

THE PRICE WE PAY, FOR OUR GUY FAWKES DAY

November 5th, is Guy Fawkes' date,
Which most of Britain, still celebrate.
In the preceding weeks,
Materials to burn, children seek.
In every district, it will be plain to see,
The disappearance of many good trees.
Under cover of darkness, some children go,
Pilfering, those 'unfortunates' soon will know.
Another dodge, these children try,
Begging for money, for their Guy.
It will be 'traumatic', for animals, come that day,
When fireworks explode, not faraway.
Fumes will affect our throat, and eyes,
When flames and smoke, rise to the sky.
Police, and fireman, will be risking their lives,
We the public, do not realise.
Families, experience pleasure that night,
Hospital staff, see many a sad sight.
Asthmatics, too will rue that night . . .

Brian Marshall

MY TREES AND I

In my soul there stands an oak tree,
From this west lands of my country
I draw the image of his beauty.
There kind and strong upon his hilltop
He holds his post and offers shelter.
Etched against the winter's sunsets.
Clothed with youthful tenderness each springtime.
Wide he casts his shade and comfort
Through the months of rain and sunshine
With the autumn comes his glory,
Swiftly shed as winter' carpet.
In my heart he twines his roots,
Through my back his strength he flows.
My arms and hands I reach out for him.

In my garden dance two birch trees,
Slender, delicate leafed and supple,
Youth and grace they hold before me.
A sturdy apple is my gift bearer,
A fragrant lilac in bridal white
Speaks of love and loveliness unfailing.

May all these trees in my life express their beings.

Z Wheeler

A Lost Idea

It was there yesterday
And the day before
I hope it's there tomorrow
For today it's no more
I thought about it last week
Or was it the week before?
An idea I had to remember things
Things that seem to slip my mind
If only I could remember
I would write it down
That's it!

Joe Bell

WISHING

I was I was a bird
So I could fly,
I would then fly up in the sky
Then as I flew
I would go over all the cities that I knew,
And the rivers that's not to be miss
And I could dive down and get a tasty fish,
Or away up in the trees
That are swaying in the breeze,
And chirp to all my friends I know
Even to the big black old crow,
I'm now so tired must get some rest
So up in the trees I go to my nest,
The nights are now drawing in
And all us birds are quiet within.

Joy Hall

UNTITLED

It's up to you my friend if on a shelf you're standing,
It's also up to you - if you're up there on the landing,
It is also up to you - if you a lighthouse keeper are,
It's up to you, if you're too warm - to leave a door a jar,
It's up to you - if an officer you be,
But even more it's up to you if the needy one is me,
I will not do it for myself while someone like you is near,
That is why I must rely on you - my own brother dear,
Of course it has to be up to you - please hear this pleader calling,
Why the heck is it up to you? Because you're so much taller!

John Leonard Wright

FOR SIX YEAR OLD MEN ONLY

I can fasten my shoes
And switch on the light
When crossing the road
I look left and then right
But it's this horrid shirt
That's my main worry
There's too many holes
For these buttons -
And I'm in a hurry!

Rita Roscoe

MISTRESS OF THE ADRIATIC

The gondola's are gay,
In a majestical way,
In Venice on the blue Adriatic.
The canals and its history
The music and mystery
And the peacefully slow moving traffic.

The Grand Canal and its story
Its wonder and glory
Of the past, the happiness and tears,
May it always resound
With its song and the sound
Of the voices of gay gondoliers.

Beautiful San Marco Square,
There's nought can compare,
With the bands, and colourful bell tower,
The pigeons, and domes,
And the palatial homes,
Once a seat of vast riches and power.

Between the water and skies,
Spans the Old Bridge of Sighs,
From the courts, to the Great Doges Palace.
Where the prisoners walked,
Heaved a sigh, never talked,
Of a sip, from a rich golden chalice.

The Venetian story of old,
May it always be told.
Of its colour, and rippled reflections,
Its richness it seems,
A true painter's dream,
A palace of few imperfections.

John Cryan

IS IGNORANCE BLISS?

Ignorance, a cushion against trouble, hurt and pain.
Ignorance, an umbrella in the rain.
Ignorance, will tell no lies, it's just a blank on face and eyes.
Ignorance is not knowing, a space between your ears, a wind blowing.
Ignorance can't harm you, no sense of doom or feeling just going.
Ignorance is bliss, so says the adage.
Ignorance blissfully presents a blank page.

S Robinson

ONE YEAR ON

It's nearly one year since you left my side,
I still cannot believe you really died.
As the day comes closer, it gets harder to see,
How life carries on but it has to be.
My heart is so heavy, no tears will come,
I exist not live, I still feel so numb.
I go to work but that gets harder each day,
I try very hard to keep my feelings at bay.
Some days are good but many are bad,
I miss you so much, all the good times we had.
Even now one year later, my door still stays shut,
I cannot go out, I'm just in a rut.
If only someone would understand,
I'm not really strong, I need a hand.
I want to cry but the tears stay at bay,
You're coping so well is what people say.
But they don't see the heartache or pain in my heart,
When I'm on my own with my memories I start.
To look at your photos and wish you were here,
Because the love we both had was so very dear.
I dread each day, I dread each night,
I dread the dark, I dread the light.
My only thought is of the one I love,
I hope you're looking down from above.
When the day is here I'll be thinking of you,
I know you'll be with me in all that I do.
Rest in peace my darling till we meet again.

Shirley Fordham

UNTITLED

I long to see the sea again,
Oh corrugated counterpane,
To fill my soul with turbulent air, as
Liquid infinity absorbs my stare.

To sit, to be and fill my ears,
With sounds unchanging through the years
Raw perspective strips me bare,
Brings salty tears to salty air.

Here I feel in harmony,
Irresolute me, irresolute sea,
My thoughts flow, only to ebb away,
Restless mass, fitful display.

The constant tumult brings me joy,
That familiarity does not cloy.
Cynical thoughts I feel dissolve,
My spirit lifts with new resolve.

It soothes the soul, it stings the senses,
Breaking down bitter defences.
I'm left in awe of God and time,
And all that by default is mine.

The sea, the poet, ceaselessly telling,
The heave and the sigh, the ebb and the swelling,
Irrepressible tide, its rhythm and prose,
Heaven scripted and composed.

Petulant pulse of a masterful hand,
A power we barely understand.
I long to see the sea again,
Oh corrugated counterpane.

Jennifer Blair

AUTUMN SUN

If I were an artist, I would paint the morning,
And wave a wand, bringing it to life.
>   It would all be for you,
>   'Tis what I'd love to do.

Autumn in the morning
Is beautiful to see.
Golds, purples, pinks, oranges and blue,
All make me think of you.

>   I see morning ever day,
>   To work, I am on my way.
>   The wonder of the sunrise,
>   In glory before my eyes.

After my day of toil,
Sorting food from the soil,
Sunset is on her way,
To say 'What a lovely day!'

>   To see each day dawning
>   Glorious the morning.
>   Then to watch it set
>   Is happiness not upset.

Barbrella

I LIVE A LIFE

I live a life, like everyone else
But I feel I'm somehow different
I go to school and say my prayers
But I know there's something missing.

I live a life, with ups and downs
Accept my monthly moods
I try not to complain to anyone
Though I know there's something missing.

I live a life, what can I do
Though there's death around me
I sleep and eat and do my work
Though I know there's something missing.

I live a life, and now I know
To look behind the lenses
Live every day to the fullest
That is now my mission.

Rhian Evans (15)

FRIENDSHIP

Stella lived in a big posh house
At the top end of the town.
Josie lived in Christian Street
And Eileen further down.

They went to school together
At the other end of town.
Castle Hill was up the hill,
The National in the town.

As kids they played together
In the big house called North How,
Sometimes down in Pigeon Well
And sometimes on the Brows.

As friends they grew together
And as friends they grew apart,
Taking different roads through life
Each following her heart.

Years flew by both good and bad
Times of joy, and sadness too.
On through life they slowly went,
Stella, Eileen, Josie Brew.

Then back they came together,
These pals of childhood's years,
Meeting in the old home town
Where memories were dear.

And just like in the early days
Their friendship still held strong,
And so it will continue
Till the sands of time are gone.

Jo McPherson

THE STONE

Upon the lonely hillside I stand
In appalling conditions
There I stand alone
Engraved for a purpose
Wind howling louder and louder
Lashing against my helpless self
The battles I have seen, so furious
Dusk falls, the night awakes
So still it is up there
Falling as the day begins
The horrific danger comes
I begin to disintegrate and rot
Prehistoric carvings,
As still as the night
Still survive
So why not me?

Thousands of years later
Here I stand
Crumbling in fear
Surviving harsh weather
So proud standing being admired
In fields of grass.

Joanna McHardy (13)

DESTINY

I do not know what's where or when
I'll try and make it to the end
But where that end may ever go
It's when I find it I will know

It may come slow
It may come fast
Maybe from the present
Maybe from the past
It will be in the future
That's for sure

My destiny is in the words
Not always rhyme
Not always verse
They are my thoughts
Not theirs or yours.

K Northrop

THE COUNTRYSIDE

Where to find,
Many treasures of the beautiful kind,
A multitude of colours, and an abundance of sound,
Where the spirit of life can always be found.

There to lie at rest and then awake,
When the sun does rise at each day's break,
Then again to blossom and to bloom,
Upon a pleasant springtime's afternoon.

Designed by God as only he can do,
Ever changing each day through,
There to welcome both the sunshine and the rain,
While for, to admire time and time again.

The countryside, this world apart,
Which as a soul and a heart,
Which mankind should adore and appreciate,
Because nature's every form of life, only God had
                    the vision to create.

David Floyd

TOWARDS THE MILLENNIUM

From 2000 years since the bringer of joy
Sainthood arising though darkness restrains
While eras of earthquake and volcano destroy
The earth is not static, its turmoil remains.

Wars and starvation the ages endure;
Peace is ephemeral, no nation secure.
Some children are destitute, some losing their lives
Man struggles, invents, enforced he survives.

Where there is love peace comes to us all
And good is transcendent whatever befall.
Time is the herald, the millennium waiting
While Earth is rotating, Earth is rotating.

E Matthews

DIGNITY AND FREEDOM

Nelson Mandela, a king amongst men,
Created a rainbow, for which most of us yen.

He's the great, great grandson of King Ngubenguka,
Who ruled their own land and were then free in Africa.

Education undertaken by an African Thembu Chief,
His resilience and hardship are beyond our belief.

The hostile reality of a white dominated nation,
Exerted on this gentle man, spiritual inspiration.

Non violent resistance to apartheid he campaigned,
Non terrorist action, but, the oppressor still remained.

Treason and sabotage were charges by government,
For this he received 27 years imprisonment.

The courageous, moral leader was at last to us released,
The oppressor's hate and anger, pray God are now appeased.

A man of vital force for racial equality and human rights,
Now the ultimate triumph 'Africa's First Black President', in sight.

He dedicates his life so the oppressed might be free,
Multi racial elections are now at last reality.

Jean Wain

HEAVENLY BODIES

Nuclear furnaces burn in fires perpetual
Perpetual? We are formed from their
Dust and ashes!

But they gaze down from the heavens with
Winking eyes. They say 'When you are gone
We will be here.'

In their ancient glare they promise
Life past death. Yet though appearing eternal
They will explode.

Still, from their shells planets ultimately
Gather, life will push up through
The death we fear.

A star burns. It pierces my seeking eyes with
Purest energy. The ray has travelled long from
Centuries past.

They shine in fiery arrested explosion. So distant
They might perish and I'd not know in their seemingly
Eternal being.

The story that came before gave birth to me
And those that shine at me in joyous existence
We are sisters.

Jacquelyn Keun

CHILDHOOD DAYS

Be it in the hills of Wales, or Yorkshire's dales, it matters not if Ulster's
Vales, kidnap the young years of your life, your childish dreams and
Childhood strife, for whatever as a child you grow, where do they go;
Gone so quickly, never slow, those days which we so deeply yearn, that
Cornish village, Scottish burn, bygone times now lost forever, but we
Will never shake that tether, which binds and grips and holds our
Souls, and shaped our futile adult goals.

Oh, how were those days, that frivolous phase, partly now a muddled
Haze, some perhaps vague reminisces, father's scolds, sweet mother's
Kisses, our mongrel Jed, long years since dead, his lolling tongue
Slavering my head, things that yet to see I crave, my wee cot bed, my
Young friend's grave, I can and will not speak for others, but I long for
Those sisters, friends and brothers with whom I played and cried and
Tarried, for whom eternal love I've carried.

But now I feel such desperation, in my abject isolation, a prisoner in
This alien nation, nostalgia burns inside me, deep and again just as a
child, I weep, my strength and hope fade and diminish, life's embers
flicker to a finish, yet, one last time those childhood faces, oh, the touch
and smell of my childhood places.
Dear mother, I beseech you, please forgive me here down on my knees
For heaven is lost, I am for hell, as I await the hangman in my cell.

Paul Jones

WAITING

It's 10.25 am.
The morning is still mauled by night,
I'm waiting on platform 6
for a train
that was due
on 2 at 5 past 10.
I'm waiting for snow
or sun,
as a bird slicing over continents
I wait,
as the regimented clock
crawls through damned minutes
I wait,
in my starvation
I wait
watching my shoe leather crack,
my nails grow,
the heart sings to a terminus,
I wait for the next shit,
for the cigarette to burn off
to light another.
I wait in silence
for the line to fall
while the covers are pulled off
at Lords,
and cars choke
the birds
over for vacation
flying
    in
       sun
         or
           snow,

As an announcement tells us
the train is cancelled,
the bus will take us
to a waiting destination
as soon as the driver arrives.
We wait,
lighting cheap cigarettes,
the dancing blue genie of smoke
mixing with lazy sweat.

Phil Jones

THAT PRECIOUS OTHER DAY

When day is done, and gone the sun
to warm some other shore,
I'll think of you at Stanton Drew,
and memories galore,
The time you said you'd love to climb
that distant hill to see
the fields and farms for miles around
along the River Dee.

It seems so strange to think back now,
to all those days well spent,
The silent barge along canal,
the boats on River Trent,
As tho' a dream I picture now
Your hair, your dress, your hat,
the precious moments of seeing you
our talk of this and that.

The words themselves were not to count,
your smile outshone them all,
But absence makes the world so flat,
and other troubles small.
When dawn is come, and up the sun,
I look across the bay
if only just to picture you
that precious other day.

Brian Nolan

FOCUS

Cold rain stings my cheeks.
Fresh winds coil her hair into copper strands
That dance around those deep blue eyes.
Rollers break around our feet
And fill the twisting necklace prints
With cream flecked foam in our wake.
I taste the salt upon her lips
As gulls glide and screech in perfect pitch.
Sebelius glows through my mind
Above the crashing waves and roaring wind
To a crescendo in the warmth of our embrace.
A deep peace runs within my heart
And runs along the sweeping cove
Until the headland melts away to tears.
Tomorrow may be shorter lived
Under surgeons skills.
But this is where I want to be
Ad all that matters are the words
I love you.

Hayes Turner

IMAGE IN THE MIRROR

It's me in the mirror, a tiny girl of five
I look at my image but I don't look right
I smile, sing, shout, cry, pull silly faces,
But the image in the mirror just stays quite still.

It's me in the mirror, a girl of ten
I look at my image but I don't look right
My hair is long and mousy
Your hair is short and sandy
I have light blue eyes, yours are dark blue eyes
We do look similar, but the image
In the mirror just stays quite still.

It's me in the mirror, a girl of fifteen
I look at my image but I don't look right
I reach out my hand to touch your face
The image goes and the mirror smashes into tiny bits
Each broken bit reminds me of my broken heart

It's you in the mirror
The image was you
My soul mate
My twin brother
My partner in the womb.

Sheila Hawkes

UNTITLED

I'm fifty in the morning
For me a new decade is dawning
But you see - this cannot be
Because inside I feel just twenty-three!

And were it not for creaking bones
And aching back
I'd surely try another tack
The image that stares back at me
Is not the one I used to see
All is changed - yet all the same
Except I now know how to play the game
It can't be right - it can't be true
Although there's nothing I can do.

I'm fifty in the morning
For me a new decade is dawning
But you see - this cannot be
Because inside I feel just twenty-three!

S Arrol

MOUNTAIN TOPS

Far distant hazy blue invitation,
'Come hither. Leave the dell,
and let me fold you in my spell.
Release your latent inspiration.
Come test your stamina and will
against my unforgiving chill.'

Nearer now the castled sky,
craggy peaks that give answer
to whisper, shout or thunder roll.
Mystically touching the very soul
with fear, with joy, with gleeful challenge
to life and limb, to overcome, to win.

Beneath the rock-strewn tumult high,
gazing upwards. Fearful
of unseen call, of mighty pull
towards the summit, perhaps to fly?
Can I? Can't I? Yes I will! With doubt,
though feared I can but try.

Now straining sinew, stretching limb
Desperate fingers cling to loosened cracks,
Taking charge of life and substance,
Insignificant, pend in space against the earthly pull
And certain death at smallest lapse.
Hold on! Hold on! Brute force or will.

The summit at last. No comfort here.
No need, there's peace, there's space, I'm free,
Of fear, of fright, relax, observe the aspen,
Timorous, trembling at wind's slight whim.
Why did I do it? Because it's there,
Beckoning, calling, 'Come test your limb.'

Richard Thatcher

THE AGNOSTIC

That lovely tree is gone, and yet
I duck my head just where
Her playful branches reached down low
To lift my hair.

The birds, bereaved, grope for a perch
Ripped from the too bright air.
Is the living spirit of the tree
Still there?

In some parallel dimension
Is the spring sky blossom laced?
Will her rich, red rug of autumn
Line the path in fruitful waste?

Does the beauty of that tree remain
Only in my mind?
Or does her presence still exist
For those not blind?

I hope there is a way in which
That lovely tree still lives . . .

Joan Page

UNTITLED

If I could be born at the age I would die
And live my life down through to 'one'
Just think of the knowledge I'd have from the start
Although life would have barely begun

I'd surely be old and my body fair worn
My hair would be thin and quite grey
But with all my wisdom I'd soon realise
That I would grow younger each day

Youth wouldn't be wasted I'd soon see to that
My brain would be so full of data
But before I grew young I'd need to find out
How to keep all my knowledge for later

Not all would be born at a very old age
It's wrong that we all should have fun
There'd be people out there with much shorter lives
So even the bad would die young

Reproduction's a problem it has to be said
Think of the pain there would be
Hard as it seems, there must be a way
To give birth to an OAP

To know from the outset how long I would live
To do all that I wanted to do
Youth would just blossom as years rolled on by
Well I can imagine, can you?

Julie Sullivan

EVENING AND DARK FALL

The moon was white as I walked on the hillside,
It stood in a sky of palest blue,
The thrush was singing his song of evening
And the long grass glistened with early dew.

The moon was gold as I walked in the valley,
It shone from a sky of darkest grey,
The owls were hooting from the far off forest
And the colours of daylight had ebbed away.

E Kay

LIFE OF A GRANDAD

As a new day dawns you awake
With a feeling of content
Knowing full well that your day
Will be enjoyably spent

After breakfast you take your grandson to school
Listening to his innocence with joy
Walking with head held up high
Remembering when you were a boy

You then join your fellow wrinklies
At the public baths
Swimming, solving the world's problems
And ending with plenty of laughs

It is now time for lunch which you enjoy
Whilst watching the news
Slowly closing your eyes and lapsing
Into a well-earned snooze

In the afternoon I return to school
To pick up my grandson
Who happily informs me that his teacher
Gave him a sticker which said his work
Had been well done.

The next hour is spent playing football
Where he gets himself really excited
As he displays his skills alongside
Shearer, Owen and Manchester United

When his parent return from work
He declares himself the winner
So I then join my wife at home
And we prepare for our evening dinner

After dinner we settle down in front of the box
To watch Emmerdale and Coronation Street
Read the evening paper, indulge in a whisky or two
Happy in the knowledge that my day
Has been fully complete.

Norman Jackson

HOME IS

Home is where hospitality is not an impossibility
Where the cold is shut out,
and the armchair embraces.

Home is a welcoming cloud of joy, relaxing and calming of nerves
Where even the darkest corner
is filled with familiarity.

Home is a bed, tailored for comfort by usage and wear,
and imprisonment for the misbehaving child.

Home is free accommodation,
Where worries are shovelled aside into a subconscious bin,
and is cherished every moment until the next working day.

Laurie Allport (13)

THE POET'S QUILL

In the corner, dank and still,
Dusty, lay the poet's quill.
Matted filaments wrenched asunder,
In penance for the poet's blunder.

The love foolish concupiscence lost
Was, for a young heart, too great a cost.
Beset by guilt for infidelity,
His despair receded to languidity.

Vowed he, ne'er to pen again,
Narration of romance's sweet refrain.
All life's pleasures he did elude,
Favouring ennuied solitude.

Thirty years stole slowly by,
Whilst life and love he did decry.
Until fate happened him one day to meet,
A girl with virtue and love replete.

Her tireless doting and attention,
Dissolved the poet's apprehension.
So slowly could be resurrected,
His emotions suppressed whilst disaffected.

The quill recovered and restored,
Again wrote verse for one adored.
An old man's lugubriosity,
Replaced by equanimity.

J F Murfitt

COME TO THIS

Black clouds cast shadows on the hills
Dark forests bend towards me
In the wind
And on the road
An old man, bending towards me.
All I see are deep blue eyes
Behind a mask of wrinkles
Blackened by countless suns.
Has it come to this?

Thoughts flicker across lips so old
And pass in the air towards me
On the breeze
And flow around me
Like the wind from where the snow lies
And eagle eyes watch like death
Over a seemingly dead country
But isn't it always an illusion.
What has come to this?

And in the fireplace, more shadows
More light in the form of flames
That lick and shimmer
Like a lion on its prey.
And the voices that carry news
Are talking somewhere on the lines
That pass invisibly around us all
Through our bodies, minds and souls.
Has it all come to this?

Summer took the train home last night
I watched her leave, and the final light
Flickered in a grey sky
Spluttering out like a sigh
On the lips of a lover who's elsewhere

And no words, touch or feeling will hold
Back the journey that they are on,
What were the words to that song?
Now it's all come to this.

Julian Bishop
Fasnakyle

WAYSIDE

The years fall by the wayside,
With a heart that is weathered by the cold, harsh rain,
Yet during those darkest winter days,
A life of old is revived,
It relieves the sense of pain.

Brighter days appear ahead,
They're not as far as you might wonder,
And if you listen carefully,
You'll hear their distant thunder.

The skies cry out,
As the frost laments,
Every man must face his crimes,
Yet without the love of a kindred spirit,
Life will leave you far behind.

When love is in the first throes of youth,
Its magic takes you to its distant lands,
To places beyond your wildest dreams,
And sometimes when you wake,
The world may not always be what it seemed.

The age-old tale,
Of joy and pain,
Together they weave their deceptive web,
The trials of life,
With all its strife,
Interwoven by the life's golden thread.

You have to believe in the power of love,
The strength of the stream that flows,
Where the tide will take you
Depends on where it leads,
And to the extent a human heart can grow.

For love is the maker
And the breaker of hearts,
For all its troubles,
Someone needs you,
Don't let it tear your world apart.

V Thorpe

MY HIGH

You stole my strength,
Now I don't know how to get around.
You picked me up,
Gave me reason.
I don't know if I told you,
But I knew I was heading down.

You give me smiles,
Miles and miles.
With you I get by,
Living so high.

Now this is my meaning,
It's something real that I believe in.
I hope you can see,
This coming from me,
It's like I mess up naturally.
I hope it's something you're understanding.

For you I smile,
Mile after mile.
I think you know why,
I never could lie.

And still we're together,
You've got me feeling so cool.
You picked me up,
Gave me reason.
You know I've said it before,
I think you think I'm a fool.

I see you smile,
For a little while.
I see you fly,
No need to cry.

Your number I'd dial,
Then run a mile.
I'm not shy,
For you I'd die.

G Real

THE RAINBOW

Again a rainbow sweeps the sky.

Red: the roses of true love, the colour I often see
in blind fury.

Orange: the colour of fruit of the warmest countries,
the colour I painted my room to escape.

Yellow: buttercups - warm sunny days - a colour
I sometimes wore in the summer of my youth.

Green: meadows and tranquillity I feel in this colour,
but also my uncut lawn and all the other jobs I must complete.

Blue: your eyes, my eyes, my best friend's eyes -
the eyes of the one I am afraid will die.

Indigo: childhood memories of school and books.
An unfamiliar entity to some.

Violet: the colour of a beautiful electric night.
A colour of reflection and wonder.

The rainbow - the promise - the pot of gold?
We live a rainbow every day of our life.

Helen Ellis

BLIND PEOPLE

Those born blind have never seen,
The sky so blue, the grass so green.
The beauty of a summer's day,
When all the mist has gone away.
The beautiful flowers blooming in gardens so fair,
Yet in their hearts do you find any care.

Their world is a world of touch,
Where love and laughter mean so much.
They can form a mental picture clear,
Built from touch and sounds they hear.

They appreciate God's beautiful things,
It seems creation to them sings.
While we who hear and see and talk,
Take so much for granted on a country walk.

Though without sight they see much more,
Than you or I have seen before.
They appreciate what God has given,
Much more than those who see.
That's for sure.

R W Cummings

UNTITLED

He spoke stuttered sweetness from his
Slowly thinking, deliberating, hesitating, mind.
Face full of concentration and eyes
That mapped her features incongruent with
What he, he . . . knew to skulk in the shifting silt.
Her eyes silently shedding the waves that shape the sand.

And like The Red Sea Parting, a thought emerged,
that she could wait to hear.

Like at a bus stop;
Knowing it will come but not when.
Only, with patience and tenderness,
For his beige eyes and hair,
And the heaviness behind his frown.
She guessed he would bring a soft gift.
Not a bumpy ride and an empty Coke can
Rattling between the seats.

Frances Easter

HUNTED, TORTURED, SLAIN

For poor foxy, staying alive isn't much fun,
Only when he has found some food is his day's work done.
He knows he has to be sneaky and plucky,
He may just catch a chicken, he may get lucky.
Mother is in the den with her brood,
Patiently waiting for the food,
Hoping that foxy will return to her,
Then they might relax a few hours without a care.
Because of farmers' dogs, the hunting was taking longer,
It was almost daybreak, and horses' hooves were becoming stronger.
Poor foxy did not concentrate,
He missed the hounds charging through the gate.
The hounds caught his scent and started barking the alarm,
Foxy appeared to be too late to save himself from harm.
Men in red coats were now charging through the gate,
When foxy heard the view halloo, he realised his fate,
His heart was beating very fast as he tried to run away.
He'd have to run himself into the ground to save himself that day.
Fleeing as fast as he could, he wasted no breath,
As he tried to escape the jaws of certain death.
His speed was becoming slower as his lungs were bursting now,
If only he could manage that hill somehow.
The dogs closed in on him, the future for foxy was very grim,
They catch him by his bushy tail, biting as they do.
Some tear at his throat, and his little body too,
They enjoy the kill, dragging his legs apart.
The huntsmen are laughing, now *why?*
Because they are surely without a heart.
The fox is dead, he was no sinner,
All he wanted was his bloody dinner.

Maureen Smith

WILD SILK

Swishing silk, wild as the Chinese rose.
Gold in all its glory with crisp elegant moves.
Twinkle, twinkle, can you see it or are you
dazzled by the strange happiness? Yes, happiness.

But green is the colour. It is in the air.
The cold air, not spring-like. Chilling green.
The monster, like a Chinese dragon.
Is this what it's all about? Being mean?

Sarah Louise Barton

THE PATH OF LIFE

The paths that we take
The life that we make
The road that we choose
The things that we lose
The people that we meet
That help us find our feet
On the road to our destiny.

The end of the line
Is just a matter of time
The road that we're on
Is it where we belong?
The road is ahead
I remember when I said
I knew I should have gone the other way.

Huw Floyd

LIGHTING THE FIRE

We all found the sitting room quite cold,
Light the fire, I was told.
I got some paper, rolled it in balls,
Next came sticks and some coals,
The sticks were laid, the match was flamed
It all flared up to a roaring blaze,
Next coal was added, and very soon,
We were all cosy in a nice warm room.

Phylis Laidlaw

MOUNTAIN GORILLA

Edinburgh, captive city,
With its castle rock,
Has a zoo where the parakeets flounce
In reds and greens and crazy blues.
The crazy blues of Edinburgh city,
Captive on its castle rock.
And the monkey chatters,
And the mynah bird's patter
Is brilliant too.
Then I come to you -
A mountainous heap of desolation,
Gazing out through your glass-fronted cage.
Dark, still, hands dangling listlessly,
Sad eyes dreaming of the rainforests of Borneo,
Weighed down with enforced indolence.
And I know that you know
That freedom
Is the only thing that matters.

Lorna Ferguson Kirk

FALSE EYES

Hey False Eyes.
Helpless, loveless eyes.
Why look at me that way?
Surely you are beautiful.
If not now, then at some point,
You *must*.
Just staring at me.
Waiting for a response, reaction
While I wait for yours, False Eyes.
I'm becoming impatient.
I can see them love everyone else,
Well, why not me?
If I have to
I will stare at them for the rest of my life.
I am going nowhere.

Liz Ward (17)

STICK 3

Once I was a pine tree
Packed into a copse,
Now I am a matchstick
Packed inside a box.
Funny how the world goes,
Dreams of liberty
Expire in curling ashes,
Now at last I'm free.

Ben Newbound

SEEING IS BELIEVING

A tiger stands by the outer door,
He's very plain to see,
'Tell them I'm here,'
He said with a growl,
But they wouldn't listen to me.

He rubbed up like velvet against them,
But they didn't feel a thing,
'Are they all dead or what?' he said,
As he bared his teeth in a grin.

He glared with his omnipresent eyes,
Then stood in a rampant pose,
'I am the tiger amongst you,' he said,
'I am standing up on my toes.'

Chatter continued of this and that,
Really it was a bore,
I laughed because nobody else could see,
The tiger that stood by the door.

'It's plainly a bid for attention,'
They said, 'She needs a positive stroke,'
That's exactly what he needs, I thought,
As I listened,
What a strangely ironic joke!

Kathleen Mary Scatchard

A GAME OF SKILL

The scene, like an immense game of chess,
She, the fair queen, to be won,
He, the black knight, my opponent
In this courting game.
The pawns, they are the people at this party,
Some there to impede me,
Others there to mingle and converse.
The black knight makes a move,
Black knight to white queen two.
I stand in stunned silence.
A valiant move,
But he has left himself open.
The game continues . . .

I move, white knight to black knight four,
Pow, he wasn't expecting that.
I break into their conversation.
My queen looks as if she needs rescuing.
'Would you like a drink?'
I say pointing to the bar.
'Mmm, thank you stranger.'
Checkmate.

Nick England

THE TRUTH ABOUT TIME

Laughter flows over and beside
My wide, strong, white ice wall.
a cold perfect sphere of snow
Begging to be thrown;
Rests lightly in my hands
Twinkling with winter
Under a white sun.

Flashing targets flicker by
And I await my chance,
                    (Which never comes).
Time melts
        secretly
                through
                        warm hands
Onto thirsty earth;
Twinkling with winter
Under a white sun.

Keyo Khan

ALONE AGAIN

I thought of you this morning,
As dawn crept through the sky.
Too numb to feel,
Too hurt to care,
But not too strong to cry.

I thought of you this afternoon.
You see, I love you still.
Eight endless weeks
Have come and gone,
No heart, no strength, no will.

I thought of you this evening,
Far on some distant shore.
I heard your voice,
I sensed your touch,
Felt close to you once more.

Patience and time will give me strength
To break these prison bars,
Unlock my heart,
Spread wide my wings,
And fly free to the stars.

Norma Fraser Reid

DREAMING OF A FIELD

My life feels like it is haunted by a waking
        dream,
One of simplicity, freedom, peace and
        love,
Always there no matter what I do or
        feel,
My safety net in the face of life's cruelty,
I am constantly dreaming of a field,
Green grass to my knees and blue sky
        reaching down,
As if in a loving, tender kiss blue meets
        green.
Sometimes I am lying on my back,
The soft earth easing my pain as I look
        skyward,
Only to see heavenly blue stretching to
        infinity,
My soul feels as if it has found its home,
One which I feel homesick for in this
        cardboard cut-out of life,
But also one which I know I will one
        day find.
Standing, arms outstretched, face skyward and
        smiling,
I turn circles where I stand,
Knowing I could never want any more,
Than I have at that moment,
Sometimes there are others who share
        my field,
But always there is me and It,
Inseparable in my imagination at least.

I don't know where my home is,
I don't know if I will ever truly find it,
All I have is a sense of destiny to guide
        me,
And my constant dreaming of a field.

Cheryl Hall

THE TRAFFIC WARDEN

Paul Small was very tall.
He gave his last ticket,
To a sleeping whippet.
The whippet awoke,
And bit Paul's throat.
Paul fell back
With blood on his mac.
A lady came hither,
All of a dither,
And found Paul Small
Dead!
Rolled up in a ball.

Leanne Nicholls (12)

DREAM LOVE

I think of you, when I awake,
you're always on my mind.
I picture what you look like,
and imagine you are kind.
You come across as gentle,
and always wear a smile,
I redden when you speak to me,
and want to run a mile.
You set me all a-quiver,
when you eyes meet mine,
But when I haven't seen you,
my heart begins to pine.
I love you from a distance,
I dare not tell a soul,
It's my own little secret,
and to get you is my goal.
But I am just a teenager,
and don't know what to do,
so when I go to sleep again,
I'll dream that I'm with you.

Coleen Clinton

LIFE

The boy screamed

He knew what was coming
As dad raised his arm
'I haven't done anything'
The boy would shout
And that would be true
But it would do no good
Dad raised his arm
He knew what was coming
Mum was screaming
She tried
But it would do no good
As dad shouted you could smell his breath
Vodka
Lager
Whisky
You could smell it really bad
She tried
She really tried
To stop him lashing out
The boy could only hide
When dad couldn't find him
He turned on mum
He turned on mum
She knew what was coming
She screamed
Thud
Then nothing
No screaming
No moving
Not a sound
Then he saw
He saw the boy
The boy ran
He tried to run but he couldn't get away
Dad raised his arm

The boy screamed
He knew what was coming
Thud
The room went silent
The house went silent
The silence was pierced by the ringing of the door bell
Once
Twice
Three times
Then there was a bang
The door flew open and fell to the floor
'What's the problem?'
Dad asked the policemen standing in the doorway
'What's the problem?'
He repeated in court
What's the problem?
Mum was dead
What's the problem?
The boy was dead
What's the problem?
What's the problem?
What's the problem?
Life.

Vicci Herbert (15)

SMART OR WHAT . . .

My son said 'Your team and mine
play each other in ten days' time.
Why don't you and Lana decide
to do some smart thinking and city linking?'

'You mean, come to the city at this time of year?'
But a negative answer Mike wouldn't hear.
He said, 'I'm sure you would enjoy
doing some smart thinking and city linking.'

I told my friend what my son had said
the idea was starting to seem good in my head.
'I'll stand in at your work, I'll drive you to town
should you decide to do some smart thinking and city linking.'

My daughter was thrilled, she loves the Dons
To see them play Hibs would sure turn her on.
'I'll have to tell them at school - if
we're doing some smart thinking and city linking.'

We took off Thursday morning, Joy drove us over
Took the 'Isle of Lewis' across the water
Lana said 'Is this real or am I dreaming?
Are we doing some smart thinking and city linking?'

Mike met us in Edinburgh, we went to the match
which proved to be more than a pleasure to watch
A draw was the outcome - how did our favourites feel
about *them* having done some smart thinking and city linking?

We went home to Michael's and home-made soup
Seeing Joyce and the family, we were cock-a-hoop.
Each minute made us more happy
to be doing some smart thinking and city linking.

Our two-day break quickly came to an end
how much we enjoyed it could never be penned.
Words can't explain how pleased we were
to have done some smart thinking and city linking.

The journey back home seemed special too
The moon through the trees sent a magical hue
I'm sure I heard that moon whisper
'Aren't you glad you did some smart thinking and city linking?'

I'll say thank you to Michael, we wouldn't have been there
if he hadn't so kindly paid half of our fare
It was a red-letter day for Lana and I
when we did some smart thinking and city linking.

C Graham

A SENSE OF BELONGING

You have reawakened the woman in me,
With your smile, caress and tenderness,
And put the sparkle back in my eyes.
The way you run your hands slowly
over my breasts,
Down my stomach, and grip my thighs,
And mount me with a sense of urgency.
As we sway back and forth,
And our bodies work in rhythm together,
You reach a climax and cry my name,
And for those few tender moments,
I know you're mine!

Debbie Hatchett

COME TO ME

Come to me when things aren't right
when shadows stalk your dreams at night,
when fear no longer stays at bay
but haunts you through your waking day.

Come to me when tears seem sure,
despair and pain is at the door,
when blackened clouds are in the skies,
then shall I gently wipe your eyes.

Come to me let me provide
a cloak of hope where you can hide,
a veil of dreams where you can stay
safe from the harshness of the day.

Come to me I'm on your side,
a helping hand I will provide
a shoulder if it needs to be
if you will only come to me.

R E Martin

SUBMISSIONS INVITED
SOMETHING FOR EVERYONE

POETRY NOW '99 - Any subject,
any style, any time.

WOMENSWORDS '99 - Strictly women,
have your say the female way!

STRONGWORDS '99 - Warning!
Age restriction, must be between 16-24,
opinionated and have strong views.
(Not for the faint-hearted)

All poems no longer than 30 lines.
Always welcome! No fee!
Cash Prizes to be won!

Mark your envelope (eg *Poetry Now*) *'99*
Send to:
Forward Press Ltd
1-2 Wainman Road, Woodston,
Peterborough, PE2 7BU

**OVER £10,000 POETRY PRIZES
TO BE WON!**

Judging will take place in October 1999